Fearless Flyer

Ruth Law and Her Flying Machine

HEATHER LANG   Illustrated by RAÚL COLÓN

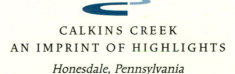

CALKINS CREEK
AN IMPRINT OF HIGHLIGHTS
Honesdale, Pennsylvania

For Mom
—HL

For beautiful Wanda—remain fearless!
—RC

ACKNOWLEDGMENTS
A big thank you to Bob Coolbaugh, retired Commander, United States Navy, and Curtiss Pusher pilot and builder, for sharing his expertise on Ruth Law's Curtiss plane and for reviewing the sketches. I am very grateful to the following readers for reviewing the text: Dorothy Cochrane, curator at the Smithsonian National Air and Space Museum, John Lyon, historian for the American Aviation Historical Society, as well as Traff Doherty, president, and Rick Leisenring, curator, at the Glenn H. Curtiss Museum. Many thanks to Elizabeth Borja, David Schwartz, and Brian Nicklas from the National Air and Space Museum for their guidance and research assistance. A special thank you to Larry Rosler for his excellent editorial feedback and for helping me develop my vision for this book.

PHOTO CREDITS
Smithsonian's National Air and Space Museum

Calkins Creek
An Imprint of Highlights
815 Church Street
Honesdale, Pennsylvania 18431
Printed in China
ISBN: 978-1-62091-650-6
Library of Congress Control Number: 2015946899
First edition
10 9 8 7 6 5 4 3 2 1
The text of this book is set in ITC Mendoza Roman Std Book, and
Thirsty Rough © Yellow Design Studio - www.yellowdesignstudio.com.
The illustrations are done with Prismacolor pencils on
Canson paper and lithograph crayon.

"When I was a little girl
I used to dream of flying, not with terror . . .
but with wonder and delight.
I would be a swallow flying south,
or an eagle swooping down from the clouds,
and then, all of a sudden,
I'd wake up, just a little girl ready to cry
because she had no wings."

—RUTH LAW

"The higher I soar

the greater freedom and liberty I feel."

The loop . . . the spiral dive . . . the dip of death!

Ruth loved to entertain folks with her daredevil tricks, but after
four years of flying in circles, Ruth longed to fly to get somewhere
. . . somewhere far away. She made up her mind to fly from
Chicago to New York City.

When Ruth Law made up her mind, there was no use trying to stop her.

Few aviators dared to fly cross-country in their flimsy flying machines. If an engine had trouble, by the time the aviator realized it, there was often nowhere to land.

Ruth had a secret weapon. She knew every nut and bolt on her machine.

"I could anticipate what would happen to the motor by the sound of it."

But Ruth also had a problem. She had never flown more than twenty-five miles. Her little biplane, built by airplane pioneer Glenn Curtiss, held only 16 gallons of gasoline.

Ruth asked Mr. Curtiss to sell her his latest flying machine. Victor Carlstrom had just flown it 452 miles from Chicago to Erie, Pennsylvania—a new American record for nonstop flight. The huge plane had a partly enclosed cockpit and held 205 gallons of gasoline, enough to fly from Chicago to New York City without stopping.

But Ruth couldn't convince Mr. Curtiss. He worried she couldn't handle the powerful machine on such a long flight.

That didn't stop Ruth Law. Her little biplane would do just fine—with a few adjustments.

She added three extra gas tanks. Now the plane held 53 gallons.

She installed a metal guard to protect her feet and legs from the frigid wind.

She charted her course, marking the mountains and hills in red ink and outlining the rivers in blue. She cut the map into strips and attached them together on a roller.

Aviation experts thought the flight was doomed. Impossible!

"What those men can do a woman can do. I can do."

At four o'clock in the morning on November 19, 1916,
Ruth dressed in four flying suits and a skirt.

The wind whipped from Lake Michigan over Grant Park
at fifty miles per hour. Her mechanics begged her to wait
until the weather improved. But Ruth had made up her mind.
The wind would give her the extra speed she needed to get to
New York City without stopping.

She took off her skirt and tucked it behind her seat. There was no need to look like a lady up where she was going. She pulled down her goggles.

Ruth was a little scared.

"I wouldn't give a cent for any experience that didn't scare me a little. The scare is part of the thrill."

At 8:25 a.m. Eastern Time, she was off.
Ruth bumped along faster, faster.

She pulled the left lever back to raise the elevators.

Her machine lifted up, up, up.

The gusty wind tossed her right, left, up, down.

"To become an aviator one has to dismiss all fear."

Slowly she gained altitude.

As quickly as the wind had gusted, it vanished. Would she have enough gasoline?

Ruth held onto the left and right levers at all times. One wrong move would send her tumbling from the sky. Holding the right lever with her knee, she turned the knobs on the map box, strapped to her leg.

"I had a tremendous feeling of freedom, of exhilaration, of power. I was steering my own course by a little six-inch map."

Dipping under clouds, Ruth hunted for landmarks: molehill
mountains . . . patchwork villages . . . lakes shining like silver dollars.

*"Each point I passed and recognized ... just made
my heart leap."*

Over Cleveland, Ohio, she checked the oil gauge: zero pressure.
Something was wrong!

Should she try to land? Ruth listened to the sound of her motor.

No clicks.
No putts.

Ruth knew her motor. It purred perfectly. So she kept flying.

The icy cold pecked through her suits.
She checked the next compass coordinates on the cuff of her glove: Erie, Pennsylvania—where Carlstrom had landed!

"I was so excited that I hardly felt the gripping pains going through my body on account of the cold."

Steering east of Erie, Ruth knew she had broken Carlstrom's record. But Ruth's excitement fizzled as the gas level dropped. If she could just make it to Hornell, New York, she could land on the racetrack.

Ten miles away her motor sputtered. Ruth looked desperately for a place to land. There was still gas in the tanks, but it was too low to feed into the engine.

Ruth tipped the plane to feed it.

Two miles from Hornell, the engine grumbled its last roar, leaving her with nothing but the silence of the wind.

"When your engine suddenly stops while you're 2000 feet in the air, it's some comfort to know that if anything can be done, you can do it."

Ruth threw the lever forward and glided.

At 2:10 p.m. she touched down in Hornell. She had flown 512 miles—
the new American nonstop record!

But Ruth's journey wasn't over. Ruth Law had made up her mind
to fly to New York City, and there was no use trying to stop her.

After refueling her plane and filling her stomach, she took off for New York City. A high hill topped with tall trees loomed in front of her.

Ruth tried to climb, but the gas weighed her down.

The trees grew closer, taller.

She steepened her path.

Branches clawed at the plane.

She held on tight . . . until all she heard was the soothing hum of the motor.

"I came as near being wrecked as I ever want to be."

Word had spread about Ruth Law. People along her flight path scanned the skies for the bird-woman perched on the front of her flying machine.

The sun dropped lower, painting the sky. Ruth squinted. She could barely read her compass. If only she had light.

New York City would have to wait until tomorrow. Heavy with disappointment, Ruth landed in Binghamton, New York.

In the morning a big crowd cheered as she took off. Soon a thick fog engulfed her. It tricked her, hiding rivers, erasing landmarks. Where was she?

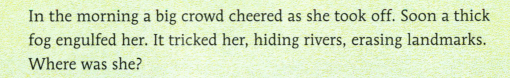

"I couldn't see a mile in front of me and that is considered dangerous in flying."

She flew lower, lower.

Coasting up hills and down into valleys.

Looking for landmarks.

Using precious gas.

At last! Port Jervis, New York. She reset her compass course.

Finally, the tip of Manhattan appeared.

The motor began to cut out.

She climbed higher, higher.

Gliding, Ruth circled around the Statue of Liberty
toward Governor's Island.

*"She smiled at me when I went past. She did! ...
I think we both feel alike about things."*

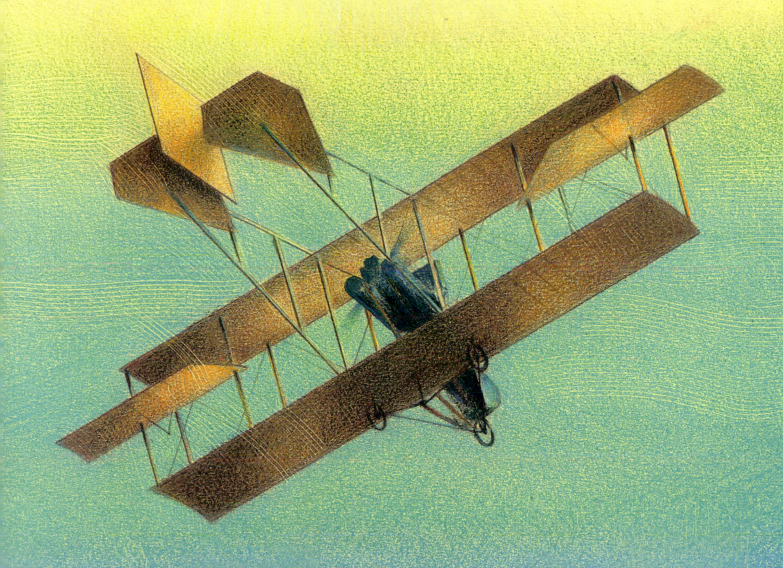

Ruth swooped over the sea wall and landed with
two long hops—straight toward a welcoming band.

She pushed down hard on the brake pedal.

The plane slowed. And stopped.

Numb with cold, Ruth didn't move at first.

Then she took off her gloves and leather helmet. Icicles dangled from her hair. She smiled at the cheering crowd. At that moment Ruth realized she had done something more important than breaking a nonstop record.

"The sky was my limit and the horizon my sphere. It's any woman's sphere if she has nerve and courage and faith in herself. She's got to have faith in herself."

MORE ABOUT RUTH LAW

SOARING IN THE WRIGHT BROTHERS' new "flying machine" was by many accounts the most hazardous adventure for a daredevil in the early 1900s. It required not only courage but also great skill. Flying in unpredictable air currents and gusts, pilots often crashed and frequently died while manipulating the flimsy planes made of wire, bamboo, and cloth. The day of Ruth's first scheduled lesson, she witnessed America's first licensed female pilot, Harriet Quimby, fall to her death from her spiraling plane.

Ignoring social norms for women, Ruth wears pants, a leather flying jacket, boots, and a cap.

Ruth never let barriers set by society hold her back. As she said, "In those days, for a woman to fly was considered a little short of ridiculous."

When Orville Wright refused to teach her to fly, she found another instructor. Ruth took flying seriously. Her husband claimed she had a special instinct that kept her safe from harm: she could anticipate what was coming. Ruth believed the key to her success was her mechanical knowledge. She spent many hours learning her plane—the engine, the nuts and bolts, the wires. She whittled struts and grinded valves until her hands blistered.

While Ruth held many records in acrobatics and altitude, her flight from Chicago to New York City brought her the most attention. Victor Carlstrom said, "I know that it takes great endurance, strength and nerve. . . . Every minute she was in the air she had to have her hands on the controls . . . her flight is the best performance to date in American aviation." Afterward President and Mrs. Wilson, aviators, and the Aero Club honored Ruth at two lavish dinners in New York City.

Glenn Curtiss sent a telegram to Ruth that read, "Congratulations on remarkable flight and new record made by you." President Wilson invited Ruth to help him light the Statue of Liberty for the first time. Thousands cheered from ships in the harbor and the shores of Manhattan as Ruth

streaked through the night sky, circling above Lady Liberty when the floodlights came on. A heavy load of electric lights strung under the wings of her plane spelled out: LIBERTY.

Ruth wanted to take her skills as a pilot to the front and fight for her country in World War I, but the US government did not allow women in combat roles. In December 1917, a Democratic congressman introduced a bill requesting that women be permitted to serve. Ruth lobbied hard, but Congress rejected the bill. Still she volunteered her time seeking donations and recruits by dropping paper "bombs" from her plane and flying at air exhibitions. The government gave her a military uniform; she became the first American woman in uniform. Ruth Law inspired many women to test their wings and challenge the boundaries set by society.

Ruth substituted Orville Wright's lever controls for the steering wheel on her Curtiss biplane. The left lever maneuvers the plane's nose up and down, and the right lever rolls the plane from side to side.

BIBLIOGRAPHY

Brace, Blanche. "Ruth Law Ends Her Flight Here." *New York Tribune*, November 21, 1916: 7.

Greeley-Smith, Nizola. "Opal from Husband's Ring, Gift on Her Wedding Day, Woman Flyer's Luck Stone." *The Evening World* [New York], November 21, 1916: 7.

Law, Ruth. "Flying With Ruth Law: My Most Thrilling Flight." *The Evening Tribune*, n.d., article in The Scrapbook of Ruth Law.

_____. "Miss Law Tells of Her Record Flight; To Try Non-Stop New York Trip Next." *The New York Times*, November 20, 1916, 1, 4.

Lebow, Eileen. *Before Amelia: Women Pilots in the Early Days of Aviation*. Washington, D.C.: Brassey's Inc., 2002.

"Nerviest Girl Aviator and Her Thrilling Feats in Mid-air." n.p., n.d. Article in The Scrapbook of Ruth Law.

"Ruth Law Arrives Here in Daring Voyage Made Mostly at 103–Mile Clip." *The Evening World* [New York], November 20, 1916: 1.

"Ruth Law Lands Here From Chicago in Record Flight." *The New York Times*, November 21, 1916, 1, 3.

"Ruth Law's Record Breaking Flight." *Flying* [New York], December 1916, 452–455.

The Reminiscences of Ruth Law (April 1960) in the Columbia Center for Oral History Collection.

"Women as Aviators." *Colorado Springs Gazette*, December 21, 1917: 11.

COLLECTIONS AND EXHIBITS

"The Biographical File of Ruth Law." National Air and Space Museum Archives, Washington, D.C., January 30, 2013.

"The Samuel P. Langley Gallery of Early Flight," National Air and Space Museum, Washington, D.C., January 30, 2013.

"The Scrapbook of Ruth Law." The Ruth Law Collection, National Air and Space Museum Archives, Chantilly, Virginia, January 29, 2013.

WEBSITES

Glenn H. Curtiss Museum. www.glennhcurtissmuseum.org.

Smithsonian National Air and Space Museum. www.airandspace.si.edu.

The Ninety-Nines, Inc.: International Organization of Women Pilots. www.ninety-nines.org.

SOURCE NOTES

Page 3: "When I was a little girl . . ." Greeley-Smith, Nizola. "Opal from Husband's Ring, Gift on Her Wedding Day, Woman Flyer's Luck Stone."